Why I Wear My Past To Work

"Chris Campbell's writing shows us that the domestic world—the human world, the interpersonal world—is not the opposite of the sublime but the very place where the sublime takes root. Stevens proposed that 'being there together is enough,' and out of this belief, Campbell makes heartfelt, compelling and deeply true poems."

—Joseph Fasano, Author of *The Last Song of the World*

BOA Editions, Ltd.

"Chris Campbell's poems mine the jewels of life from the sudden raw dark of serious illness. They take in *The View from a (this) hospital window* and look back from the brink of mortality and its bare bones. He finds beauty in the small occasions of boyhood and parenthood from both sides, learns even his *father once had long hair*. They take place in holiday rockpools and childhood homes.

Chris deftly recovers himself from disintegrating language to face up to the tyranny of time. He learns to be …*the man I wanted to be that the six pack / PhD or six figure salary* don't matter so much, that it sometimes rains. And yes, it's ok to dream of the care-free life of a cowboy away from the untidy demands of parenthood (for one night only). This collection is a celebration of life from a poet who knows its worth and to *Pluck the present / Hold it close to my chest/ just for the moment…*"

—Martin Figura, Author of *The Remaining Men*

Cinnamon Press

"This impressive collection of poems strums the heart strings, composing moving melodies of meticulous metaphors and sentiment filled similes. A beautifully edited collection showcasing beautifully unedited stories, exposing the realities of living out expectations and dreams. Chris Campbell candidly shares a perspective we so rarely get told of. The narrative unravels like a film reel, projecting his fleeting moments and forever memories into your heart. It is an empathy encouraging, effortless read where the eye falls from one line to the next. Chris' level of observation is extraordinary; he doesn't see people and places, he sees into them. The poems uncover genuine gratitude for life, love and those he has lost, reminding you that, even when static distorts the full picture, 'life's still worth tuning in for.' A nature-noticing, thought-provoking, heartbreaking, joyous, wholesome, transparent and vivid read. An all-consuming sensory experience of beautiful dreams, harsh realities and silver linings."

—Jemima Hughes, Author of *Into The Ordinary*

Verve Poetry Press

"This gem of a collection is a finely crafted meditation on family life and a testimony to the changes wrought by fatherhood. There are filmic moments of crisis or tenderness, and in a section about ill-health, moving descriptions of hospital life. These poems take us into a house crowded with toys, and show us tiny poignant moments between father and child.

Bittersweet lyricism, and a wry humour, pervade the entire collection. The poetry is never less than delicate, but its sheer emotional heft will catch you unawares."

—Lesley Curwen, Author of *Rescue Lines*
The Hedgehog Poetry Press

"From the first poem Campbell writes a life which could be considered normal with an attention and curiosity that those considered normal are neither required nor expected to display. The sensibility is quiet but alive, with the poet's sensitivity to the keynotes of life always present but rarely overshadowing the quotidian. This is not poetry which describes the routine only to show how it disintegrates in the face of a deeper truth. In these poems, as in life, the unimaginable and the ordinary co-exist. This approach is a perfect match for the subject matter. The book hinges on its second section in which the poet's health fails him; the awareness of mortality then shapes our responses to all the poems.

In a world of books which want to devastate you, Campbell is content to remind you that you could at any moment be devastated. He allows you to carry on with your day— for now at least. This is a quiet momento mori of a book full of love, regret, curiosity, inevitability, and truth."

—Tom Sastry, Author of *Life Expectancy Begins to Fall*
Nine Arches Press

"Campbell captures the minutia of the world in exquisite detail. These are personal, humorous and poignant poems rooted in the tragi-comedy of daily life.

His snapshots of moments, landscapes and characters are skillfully and empathically written. They linger in the mind of the reader, demanding to be read again."

—Kitty Donnelly, Author of *In Dangerous Hours*
Indigo Dreams Publishing

"Chris Campbell's *Why I Wear My Past to Work* is a luminous, heartfelt collection that gently uncovers the profound within the everyday, offering a quiet mysticism that invites the reader to meet each moment with curiosity, gratitude, and awe. With crystalline craftsmanship and emotional depth, Campbell transforms domestic scenes; parenting, home life and work, into exquisite verse. Fatherhood, masculinity, and working life are explored with rare honesty and grace, turning memory into a form of witness that is both intimate and universal, infusing the quiet poetry of domestic life with lyric enchantment. The result is a collection that feels deeply personal and fiercely true - an extraordinary addition to an already impressive body of work."

—Samatar Elmi, Author of *The Epic of Cader Idris*
Flipped Eye Publishing

"Chris Campbell's playful, lyrical second collection, *Why I Wear My Past to Work*, interrogates aspects of life that we so easily take for granted and transforms them into rich tapestries of experience: in his artful, deft hands, the ordinary and mundane become intriguing, extraordinary. Here's the supermarket queue, office, steam-room, hospital ward, seaside outing, pub, bathroom and children's birthday party, where incidents thrive as Chris casts his gaze on people, objects and places in language charged with inventive imagery, wit, irony and empathy. Here are the pleasures, chores, routines, clutter, joys and frustrations of domestic, social and working life: at bathtime, a toy rubber pufferfish stretches a trans-Atlantic friendship; a pair of trainers 'have an ecosystem /of their own.' Memories, 'the whispering waves of {the} past,' leap suddenly into the present, such as a burst tyre on the M6 releasing a stream of recollections of childhood trips to Scotland; they take us to a deeper level before fading in the face of a transformed, often tender, sometimes self-mocking, often wry, awareness of the present. In a style that sits easy on the ear, Chris unleashes the power of precision of detail and language. The colloquial turns into the arresting. The odd becomes beautiful. The taunting frustrations of life wriggle with humour. *Why I Wear My Past to Work* is an uplifting, hugely enjoyable collection that will have you lingering on individual poems, re-reading them, but wanting to devour more. Already, I can't wait for Chris's third collection to appear."

—Robert Walton, Author of *Sax Burglar Blues*
Seren Books

WHY I WEAR MY PAST TO WORK

WHY I WEAR MY PAST TO WORK

Chris Campbell

PARLYAREE PRESS

Parlyaree Press
Atlanta, Georgia
www.parlyaree.com

Library of Congress Cataloging-in-Publication Data
Names: Campbell, Chris, author.
Title: Why I Wear My Past To Work / Chris Campbell
Description: First Edition | Atlanta : Parlyaree Press, 2025
Identifiers: LCCN: applied for | ISBN 9781961206182 (paperback)
Subjects: LCGFT: Poetry
LC record available at https://lccn.loc.gov/

Interior & Cover Design by Parlyaree Press

Front Cover/Title Typeface is 1942 Report by Johan Holmdahl & Bulletin Typewriter. Interior Text Typeface is Baskerville. Cover and Interior Imagery Licensed for use.

Print ISBN: 978-1-961206-18-2
Ebook ISBN: 978-1-961206-19-9

To Rowa, Laith and Jude and all your joy.

WHY I WEAR MY PAST TO WORK

Chris
Campbell

TABLE OF CONTENTS

SLEEVE JEWELS

IT RAINS TULIPS

SIX-FIGURE SALARY

LUNCHTIME SUITS

Sleeve Jewels

No Cufflinks at My Company Awards

My son packs floorboard cracks
with my sleeve jewels.

When we moved to this house
we feared he would crawl in dust—

deep cleaned every room to no avail.
But he points out dirt to mop.

He snatches my cufflinks again,
parades them in his playroom.

Only hands them back for milk
or a fairytale.

In the hotel before an awards night;
bow tie, a milk-tipped crayon—

I check my pockets. No jewels to be found
as my sleeves hang.

Are they at the bottom of his mug,
lined up on a racetrack with his favourite trucks?

When he spots their hexagonal outline
he will snicker, fling them in the air,

as I ask a stranger to tie my cuffs
with the string from an eye mask.

Ode to a Rubber Pufferfish

You swallow bubbles, squeal, spray
waterfalls over my son's curls,
inflate memories greater than Yosemite Falls,

collide with lavender bombs. Laith's grin
flashes, floods tiles with treasure.
I splash you, yellow pufferfish, tiny

buoy drifting through shampoo wake.
On holiday with friends in California,
we fished you from their garden pool defiant

you were ours. But as bath time tunes
unfold at home, we discover two waterfalls—
toes circle, foam erupts—

for that one evening before we post
you seawards to San Francisco, to paddle
adventures with other kids; bobbing

through birthdays, barbecues. A souvenir
of our trip, from pool to bath,
you return like summer.

Ode to the Pruning Woman Eaten by Vines

Google Maps fails and I slam the brakes,
swerve to skirt your wild lawn, the curves
of your glamourous dress; worms squelch

through sequins. You're too busy to hitch
your limbs; strips of spiked hair prick from under
a wide-brimmed hat, cheeks half buried

in pruning, gloved fingers sprouting earth.
A mesh belt tucks in your remaining hours;
fruit clings to pots and you rise

to let watering-can sleeves tip. Sun bakes
your freshly painted villa. I wind my window
down and in air-conditioned splutter tell you

I'm late for my son's birth. Your brambling tongue
feeds me directions, and I screech away, decay
fumes. In the mirror I see you wilt,

then turn again to water, ensuring the survival
of roots – buckets of lawn luscious and full
as I hope your life has been before you feed

your veins to the soil, before your best attire
spoils, threads unravelling like climbers, before
your road ahead is swallowed by sun.

When Our Child Drops a Toy at Cheltenham Spa

A train halts by hanging baskets
and the rain pelts—flowers whistle in June.
Vacant queues of passengers; pairs in tune.
I call to check your progress.

You make the platform step with our child,
spiced perfume trails.
You could be in any provincial town.
Your short scarf thawing your peaked shoulders,

you wear pumps for grip,
our son wrapped to your chest.
But today, underneath cloud columns,
as a sheepdog finds respite under a bench,

no one helps you lug: the pram, suitcase,
three large shopping bags, and rucksack with toys
clutching either side. No one aids you up mountains
to the exit, through the ticket barrier,

out the station and onto the bus.
You phone to let me know you're fine
and on your way, as I hug the guilt.
You haul the mass, hoist it onto the luggage rack,

not a crack from our toddler until he wakes
and cannot pat his shaggy dog.

Watching My Wife at Three Cliffs Bay

You soothe rock edges
with your twinkling swimsuit,
adore our son—he titters into moats,
kids in the waves glance back.

I crouch in a rock pool—
whelks for toes, watch you net the sunset,
grow taller against the tide,
arrive with the current under your armpits.

I catch fresh eyes in the ocean
gazing at near-finished castles—
built then sunk over generations.
Pupils plead to play with our buckets.

We clutch ancestors' hands,
mould turrets with Laith,
face the whispering waves of past:
we're bolder as our castles rise.

I hum over seagull squawks
serenading our sandwiches,
my salted lips,
breath heavier than the gale

now whistling of foundations we've made.
Laith lifts high his bucket and spade.

My Son Grows as I Regress

My chores spread—
with piling pots of plant-based yoghurt.

I stumble over my toddler's Crocs,
screech from piano stool

to long-life milk,
tread on his latest bear and its tedious tunes.

Spill laundry detergent onto his nappy bin
next to discarded egg and soldiers.

Pats on the brow from my wife as I sprawl.
Ceiling lifts, my cheeks rattle into rashes.

I cast the pushchair's straps
to hook odd socks.

Babble into rice cakes
now I revert to tantrums,

re-live my own spurts;
will I tell my son one day?

He says *duck* and quacks.
I pluck my hair as I wipe pesto from his.

We spot feathers on the lawn, buttercups,
there are more teeth in his chortle.

The Sea Steals Our Picnic Blanket

and returns cling film cleansed. Scrub
your fingertips in the fairy-liquid waves,
my captured goodwill floats away in our lunchbox.

At the scene of the crime you tilt your soaked
face to evict ear-squatter sand, ask why
I had positioned us so close to the sea. Shells prise

my protestations. My eardrum bursts, wax surfs
on pulsing waves. Jellyfish fireworks
sting the sky. Rocks thud like bailiffs:

I'd dragged our blanket, four-course platter
and cava down to the shore. A downpour
threatened, even the tide was leaving.

But in a final assault it nicked our basket:
a week's wages feeding the fishes. My wrists
freeze under my seaweed-soaked shirt.

Your pupils are beads from the seabed
drawn by nature's net. I want to pick
at your best bits, before you leave again:

this open shell won't close.

Why I Can't Sleep in This Chameleon's Moonlight

Chameleon darts from torchlight
across this Cyprian wall,

scuttles far above my sun hat,
spies my peeling forehead from

its 360-degree viewpoint.
I'm sure it was the same one that was racing

along the water tank at lunchtime –
ducking from photographs,

weaving away from my sketches.
Willing me not to capture

this land and its inhabitants;
the island's nature that fires

my thoughts once I force my daze
on dust-smeared pillows,

stirring for what isn't mine.
I, who can't sleep

next to this pool of holiday moonlight,
wish to scurry too,

for the dark is soft
and the torch's glare exposes guests.

We Meet in Attic Bar for My Stag Do

I have never struggled for anything
more than sunlight punches through
this blind. Not even in journalism exams

that I took again and again, nor racing
along the Thames at the weekend.
My trainers have an ecosystem

of their own. My fiancée shuns them.
I know one day I'll run again,
pass the veg store and pharmacy,

the pie shop and spaghetti cafe,
the graffiti-wearing Church of God
with adjoining nursery.

For my stag do, we meet in Attic
on the corner, next to The Bearpit
roundabout. You tell me how you still

miss London. In PR now after years
of journalism. Both of us older.
Someone broke into your flat and stole

your laptop. We miss newspapers.
We are always competing with time.
Buses pass like swans in lunchtime traffic,

pick up passengers like crumbs.
We compete for attention
until we no longer need to.

It's fine to just sit here and reminisce.
Watch the light jostle, wonder
when we'll meet again.

How This Cuban Shop Serves Pachanga

He left Cuba and opened this store,
with its pulses, nuts and flours.

Upstairs, a coffee bar; his welcoming
daughter deep in lunch specials—

pisto; curries; chimichangas; enchiladas.
Spices soak up a wet July,

turn this cafe into Cuba
quicker than the tables they wait.

As Spanish and African roots
vibrate against menus, pachanga lifts

the floorboards and customer smiles
below. He must miss the mountains

and forests of his island—now captured
in framed paintings—after 30 years.

But this place is the result.
The owner of the toy shop next door,

also open for three decades,
points punters towards his friend;

this hidden gem. *You can't beat
those enchiladas.* Camaraderie keeps

these independents open; holding hands
down the high street in a mambo.

Day Trip, 2000

You grin in fading sun, checked shirt
and flattened hair. Were we on Exmouth Beach?
That's how I remember it. Sunhat, ice cream,

your gums revealed like mine are now,
frowning at this photograph. Remembering,
how an hour before, we were on the boat

eating lunch, and, as young boys do, I grew
restless counting the passing geese, while you
discussed your final plans with Mum.

You called me a *little bastard* and I stomped
my feet and dragged a napkin towards the deck.
Your eyes were larger than the fish of the day.

Did I cause a scene? Maybe. How was I to know
it would be the last time we'd see you, uncle?
I'd clenched the napkin thinking *bastard, bastard.*

We Are All Anarchists...
After You Drop Your Elderly Mother Off

Punks parrot corporate niceties
on my doorstep.

They pogo on the kerb,
merchandise in hand,

bang on about the heatwave
and their elderly mothers.

Off goes one in his squashed
Suzuki, his wife seals sales fodder.

Anarchy... just after they drop off
their 80-year-old mum at the bingo.

Spit on cracked tarmac,
next to manicured gardens—

no future cares while they gaze
over fertile hills.

These punks wanted to live
for a few decades, now they demand

their triple-lock pension.
They've swapped pills for cabbage,

absinthe for tea.
I'm an anarchist too...

when my kid's away
and it's a bank holiday.

It
Rains
Tulips

The View From This Hospital Window

I admire an empty bench for hours—
then a glum couple sit to share strawberries.
A pensive man pats his Jack Russell.

Yoghurt white sky; life's brighter now.
I slurp weak coffee, push away the lunch tray,
read tv listings.

Through the door, I hear nurses ponder patients—
my name. I stand
as glass amplifies the sun.

Today I Can't Speak

              I   speak
today—   did I think   that?
Can't   can't   speak
 speak today, or
did   did   I repeat it?
Dr gave me a   note   note
says   I'm I'm   confused,
but it takes two   doctors
before a brain scan.   They thought
that's   the way   I   am am.

In the Queue at Bristol Royal Infirmary

It's F-O-L-T-I
the A&E patient
states in gruff voice.
What's faulty?
asks the nurse
behind a glass screen.
No, FOLTI!
Sorry, what's not faulty?
Mr Folti points to his throat,
claims he's in severe pain;
cannot swallow.
What's your name?
He spells it out, I catch every
other letter as he coughs
in frustration.

I wait my turn,
the only thing I'm sure
of in this world
as I'm asked my address,
how I got to the hospital,
is Mr Folti's name.

Holed up After Hunting for a Gift

I order tulips for my wife's birthday,
lounge like a seal on my hospital chair.
When they are delivered

I'm sent a photograph
of the box in front of a steel
shutter, a handrail beside it.

I show the screenshot to a nurse,
lap the building,
find every handrail in the vicinity

as if on a visitor trail—check out this
20th century staircase since decorated
with chewing gum.

I leave reception with my picc line—
revolving door stuck
like conversation. Swaying in my nightgown,

as unapologetic as a curtain twitcher.
I tour the grounds – cancer block,
children's centre, A&E—

find security guards huddled like penguins
beside a car park, show them the photo.
Nothing. A suggestive flipper.

I stumble to a warehouse;
the parcel delivery point.
Bird squawks—I would not care

if it shits on me. Cold pinches my elbows.
I resign after my hour search,
head back towards bed.

I pass the coffee shop, hear my name
My consultant, eyebrow raised,
looks at my phone and calls

over the receptionist: a pouncing leopard.
They hunt with me through the corridors,
side entrances. Fruitless.

The day after my wife's birthday
the flowers arrive. A hippopotamus
of a porter delivers them.

Soggy petals line the storm-cloud
floor. The gift tag is now out of date.
Even when I'm holed up it rains.

After Leaving the Ward

I ease into the park next door,
clasped in sun, with a low white cell count.

Who's that feeding crows his lunch?
He hums to Radio 4

clutching his portable receiver,
with damp sleeves, clotted hair.

I cross a bridge, cars pass slow as clouds,
a scene from The Archers fades between drills.

Construction workers beep for pedestrians to move.
Dramatic interlude as they refuse.

I think back to those cocooned
on my ward,

blinking as medical devices beep.
Their bed pans cleared by strangers.

I wish to be a digger,
to lift them, to be the wind

blowing laughter into their card-cluttered corners,
to be the crow's caws to remind them of sky,

to be their top radio show so
they know life's still worth tuning in for.

There Is a Mortuary on the Horizon

I watch hearses pass my house.
One overtook the other yesterday.
I wonder what it means. Dead crow

in my garden, solemn tunes
every time I turn on the radio.
The door thumps in dull beats,

I open the scratched wood,
revealing lilies on the wall,
light through the gap

like a coffin lid. The guest is all
in black, speech in hand along
with his handkerchief.

I feel cold in my bones, no meat
left today, the kitchen pipe's rotten egg
stench covers me, laying to rest

in my pale nostrils;
the drain has not been fixed
in years. My waxed expression ushers

my visitor away with his religion.
Shine of his shoes unbearable.
I have never been one to plan my own funeral;

no colour, no playlist, no dessert.
Another hearse. There is a mortuary
on the horizon, where the traffic ends.

A Church Waits

Next week it will wake anew;
pews full with Sunday ties,
ribbons in hair, fresh passion flowers
blossoming with chatter.

But for now, stained glass waits against stone,
the choir creaks, worn bell ropes hang
in prayer, the names of lives lost
ready to be read.

Then bells, the church door clunks,
wine and wafers, the crack of knees.
This church rings in service,
spirits warm the gardens.

You Play the Violin on Your Mum's Birthday

I sift through old receipts,
car finance letters.
Then the odd card from Dresden.

Here are photos of your husband
and sons on the beach by the Baltic Sea.
A bookmark from a John Constable exhibition

from your time in Ipswich.
After we met in Surrey we'd dance
to Blues on Wednesdays.

More bills and a phone contract.
When thumbing through this box
of paperwork it rains inside.

Your tale of playing the violin
for your mum's birthday is the
sun enveloping the clouds.

Did You Return Our Birthday Gift?

I ponder my former colleague's operation,
watch peonies persist against a growing storm.

The postie knocks,
returns the birthday gift we sent last month,

his bag planted on weed-held steps, letters overflowing
like a bad argument.

Any day now:
my ex-colleague's long-awaited procedure.

Her package weathered
as if it has been dug from the earth,

her address scrawled out
like it never existed.

No house number, postcode,
the tracker receipt is long gone.

I recount the times we traded
lunch to proof publications.

The postie uproots his sack,
picking envelopes off the ground.

If they stick, will we be here forever?
Will we get our flowers back?

Mr James' Aim When He Retires as a Surgeon

I stalk my best friend's surgeon.
He adores photography and blogs about nature.
He posts about holidays, his post-work
jollies. I bet he has a big house.

When she's on the table
and his favourite ballads choke the theatre staff,
I pray his passions align,
that he puts all into the task in hand.

His photos apparently hang
in the personal collections of famous musicians.
It will be his retirement career.
Don't tell his patients.

I'm a Turtle Hiding its Truth

within a beach cave.

The kitchen wallpaper could dry
quicker than I move—

I wish to groom my shell and hurtle
into the Mediterranean Sea.

But my legs are cracked eggs;
I'm lost on this tiled floor.

I remember many romantic dinners
as I drag myself towards countless waves.

The sink is full with last night's plates,
rotten scraps blocking the pipes,

I brush off the circling *kack-kack-kack-kacks*,
switch lights off to hamper predators.

Ten years earlier I nearly lost you in this sand,
no matter how fast I try

I can't navigate life's hurdles alone.

Why I Wear My Past to Work

My wife escapes our house for work,
even the shower sobs—

all that is left of our honeymoon are photographs.
I step over suitcases we bought in our youth,

the shutter yawns above the broken
radiator. I open it to reveal dog walkers,

chores to do now.
I mould my life around our broken taps;

the showerhead drips after me
to the bus stop, past the newsagent's and post office.

It leaks beside me at my desk.
Only I notice the puddle.

Six-Figure Salary

Revellers Howl in the Fine Hours

His makeshift stick flicks empty wrappers
from the kerb, I want to capture him in a feature
for work. The aid bounces alongside his berberis
legs—a sniffer squirrel for litter.

He clears his morning path but there's no pride
with all these remnants from a heavy student night—
clematis would bloom and wilt before then.
Crooked scooters map out the trail that the revellers

howled in the fine hours. The old gent waits by a bus
stop to let the strollers pass, his eyes flower
as kids chase, snatch at each other's doughnuts
among the plant pots, blueberry jam and van fumes.

I see him counting his years amongst shrivelled leaves
that swallow daylight—elbow pads and braces
bare decades. I skip to my office past sobering sights;
shops asleep, bars like strangers.

Uncloaked trees stretch to birds: skeleton fingers.
Yer late, bawls a homeless man, ukulele in hand.
I nod and speed up. I'd usually stroll after that, but I don't,
instead beat that last week into deeper potholes, and faster

than my press releases. Band posters headline frosted windows,
arguments break out on ice. I halt outside my work
building, wipe media enquiries from my forehead,
tighten my belt ready for another day in PR, and who do I see…

the elderly man, tall with his stick—surrounded
by leaves blowing away tomorrow.

Five Schoolboys Pick Pyracantha

berries from behind a broken wall.
They inspect their goods then rocket

the passing scooters, a shoulder shrug away.
Red palms under woollen gloves, the ones
their folks forced upon them after breakfast.

These kidnappers who infiltrate such
well-kept lawns. I recognise one of the troop—
he was pointing out the pharmacy to an elderly

couple, before pelting them with his handful.
Or is he feeding the present to passers-by?
Pockets of autumn reminding there is life

on this road; this jolly gang, serenading October
after class. Chestnut sleeves, sherbet deodorant;
their firethorn fingers paint houses with sunset.

It is Autumn Again

the leaves are old friends.

Do you remember when we skipped
on this bandstand?

Horse chestnut smoke wrapped around us
like scarves, your coat a bright bonfire.

I hear children snorting into candyfloss.
Pigeons have taken all they can to nest,

would have your earmuffs if they could.
We talked about upcoming exams,

why art was your favourite subject.
Your boots as heavy as the sky.

We threw sacks at tin cans to win
a teddy neither of us wanted.

Everything seems difficult now
as I take your life to the charity shop.

A Cat's Garden

I paw a ball of sunlight;
atop this rough stone wall,
survey my lawn and spread
my pads like butter.

Beside my bobble hat belly,
my tail conducts the falling sun.
Bees hum, thicken
the congested box hedge.

I take minor interest:
the evening honey drips.
When all else hides in shade,
I rest on my spotlit throne.

The kids' slide has fallen—it's never
picked up. Empty bottles clang,
a sock is discarded
on grass like an insult.

The owners have ruined this spot,
shooing me away
with their musical renditions,
screech-filled dinners.

But the strangest thing of all
is the regular visits
of injured pigeons—they hop up
and down the steps. It's a sign.

When I take their heads,
their tombstone torsos
crowd the back door,
I hear folks mourn another chore.

A Helping of Sand After University

I snatch laughter when I hear it,
crunch old jokes one by one,

gnaw on childhood holidays—
pick at postcard sentiments.

I snap the despair of part-time jobs,
peck at tiffs with exes.

Clamber through every hour
to pluck the present—

hold it close to my chest
just for a moment.

I swirl prospects
chugged since university,

smear lost companions whose names cling
to the corners of my grimace;

I gurgle their nicknames by rocks
so even whelks know.

As I wait for dessert of sand
and tomorrow, I thank clouds—

people rarely do—
for their contribution;

for this meal, for the softness
of rain, for the future.

What a Cearense Man Asks Me in the Steam Room

I own all the answers,
flat in my back pocket.
I snatch at them in the gym,
lose sight of them
in the steam room.

Back at a bier fest, I met an old
school friend for the first time
in 15 years—when he raises his hand
we're in Maths class,
making practical jokes at the teacher.

Now in eucalyptus, a Cearense
man asks: *Ever been to Fortaleza?*
Know about the crime there?
What it's like to be held up
at a cash point? I don't respond

between questions, just stare
at neon lights searching for answers.
Didn't have any in Maths either,
or when my pal asks what I've done
over the last decade.

Is having two children enough,
buying a house, making it to the gym,
never going to Brazil?
I find the answers briefly,
keep them in my grasp.

Content that I know everything life can offer—
that it's all cyclical and I've done it before.
Until I'm thrown again
by a stranger, mate from the past.
They escape like steam.

I Drown During an Awards Do as the Queen Dies

News breaks of the Queen, I sink
into a London pub off Oxford Street

with a colleague spouting discontent
over cuts in journalism. He's a republican,

neutral on the draw of her smile, but I've drifted
from shore with the tide, without the life jacket

of a queen you could seize at any moment,
all your life. I shiver as we wash up

at the awards night we're in the capital
for, to mark the armed forces. What a place

to be, after the announcement.
On stage: muted chats though those mourning draw

comfort from being surrounded by military
who served for queen and country.

Covering the night for work, I rally
a former soldier active in Afghanistan

when he was 19. He throws speech grenades,
shoots off about the dead bodies he saw,

his contempt for the Taliban and Muslims. After storms
of award presentations—a trawl of stuttered applause—

I tell him my wife and I are Muslim.
His tongue dries because I'm white

and had nodded as he recounted.
He'd killed, since done everything to forget,

started new work—now has a one-year-old
daughter—reiterating he'd been young

and had rescued his mentality since. He doesn't
win an award. They cancel the band

but the audience cries the national anthem.
I hope high tide returns

even without her smiling blue eyes.
Plaudits for those lost on their own seabed,

grieving in their own way—the slow rising of flags.
God save the unseen.

Rescue

My bonfire breath: a smoky hiss sharper
than the bottle edge that bursts our tyre
on the M6 down from Glasgow.

My wife and I on the verge with our son
who scuttles after me as I hunt
for civilisation. Minutes hang

from the strings on his snowsuit.
Rescue on its way, I clear the boot,
remove the spare wheel.

Son roars throughout. Our car goes
through a lot. My father's did too.
Once, we were glued to a gusty hillside

trying to reach the Duke of Sutherland—
my grandmother's maiden name.
Orange peel skies after our Distillery trip.

Our wheels sank, a clear drop beside us.
The recovery man and I ripped up earth
to create space for the tow truck.

Have yer lost yer 'eads? he bellowed
into the bubbling dusk.
My dad would drive us

up to Scotland to visit grandparents.
My mum handing us hard-boiled sweets.
I'd thrash with my brother

for which side to sit. We'd pinch
our pillows, Game Boys for hands.
I'd muse on how Dad would drive

until the warm caramelisation of day
left only the flare of brakes.
We'd cheer as we crossed the St Andrew's flag,

eyes peeled on splendid glens
and Highland cattle. More scenic roads
than I now have years, and wild berries painted

to parts of our car otherwise forgotten
like wet washing in a storm.
We watched the truck vanish with our worries.

Even though you are a short journey
or phone call away, I always see
your face, Dad, etched into the moon.

The Meadow, Dugdale Avenue, 1993

For Simon Ballard

Your golden hair would tail
in a triangle at the back,
above your Manchester United collar, upturned,
marked with grass, streaks of mud stains.

At night, tittering over walkie-talkies,
we'd share what was keeping us awake:
a creak from the wardrobe, the dark
from under the stairs.

We last met eight years ago
for pints in a pub near our old school.
I met your wife and newborn daughter,
we spoke of distant friends, how we got lost in Prague.

I still picture you in the sixth form corridor,
skateboard in hand, chain on pocket,
how good you were at Physics,
how we'd be kicked out of German for chatting.

Outside the common room,
with its Bob Marley poster,
photos of previous class years hung neatly in rows
like our ambition on pegs.

I check my phone to read over our final messages:
we said how much time had passed.
I moved away before you did, now you've left before me.
I was going to text you to meet soon.

As boys on our backs in the Meadow,
we'd follow murmurations with our fingers,
spit out strawberry bubblegum
at cries to go home for tea.

I'd swap all future wins
to take my football back among the dandelions,
to lie on our muddied jackets and bikes,
watch the starlings fall and rise.

I Am the Man That I Wanted to Be

minus the six pack,
PhD or six figure salary.

I am the man that I wanted to be.
I work all night, eat junk food,

watch tv. All my friends
have moved abroad or married.

I am the man that I wanted to be,
haven't picked up any new

skills, languages, I'm stuck
on YouTube videos late

into the night. Drive my mediocre
car to the weekly shop,

blame all my problems on the
political system.

I am the man that I wanted to be.
With healthy kids, a beautiful family.

Halloween as a Father

We knock on doors: your first trick cr treat.
You say, *one day you'll be a skeleton, baba.*
I clock my pumpkin painted hands,
then yours, while we fright in porch light
waiting to roar. *A really scary one,*
you add, fists full of chocolate.
In your grin I spy resilience; teeth that you will lose,
only for more to come.
I wish my bones could lie.

Bin Workers Wake You

You swoop under the covers,
with a favourite crayon,
then pretend to sleep—

oblivious to the world
until the clang of bin workers.

Suddenly we stand, you point:
Truck! Follow the beeps down
the road with your finger.

Minutes whisk light, dawn
reveals its chosen palette;
wrens flit against pink and orange.

Now you are ready to skydive
into the day:

Truck! you repeat. *Again?*
 I summon it back
with the birds and sunrise.

Lunchtime Suits

Who Gave Our Kids Glitter Stickers?

As I slide across this jelly-smeared floor
—remnants from my child's birthday—

I clock the exit and pour the rain into my hood.
My parents reminisce with old

university friends, our new Bristol
mates orchestrate survival tricks.

The cry for more songs echoes as my two-
year-old orders around his toy double decker

and us to accompany his nursery rhymes.
I close my locked jaw, count fresh bodies lining

up for cake crumbs. Patience fills
mouths—silent seals, belly full of bills—

let's just lie here and flail like tots:
a bob of wardens breaking social laws. This crime

of overstaying our time slot when the next party
is due; baristas gesticulate. Line us up against the hot

falafel and couscous. I bulldoze kids' gingerbread
houses; soggy after 7UP sprays

from abandoned party hats. Twinkle, Twinkle, Little Star
never better than when a choir of screams

explodes. At least no one's escaped onto Horfield
Common. Only two stray dogs appear during the whole

three hours and those with a phobia return
from under the table. Another balloon pops, the speaker

declares it has low battery. We haul rubbish
into waiting parked cars. I peel tractor stickers

off the floor—whose idea was it to share them out?
Why don't we just stay here forever, join the next

occasion—a birthday—or a wake?
Glittery stickers will brighten it up. Let's wait

and maybe our little ones won't age at all—
the candles won't blow out.

Shove Your 3-for-2 Flyer

My bike tyre could inflate
of its own will before I'd bow
to your 3-for-2 fast-food offer. We live

sustainably, don't you know? Toppings pile
on drains, tiny council boxes can't hold
the hundreds of empty bottles

the weekend drank.
When the wind comes I hear them whistle.
In heavy afternoons they escape—

roll their way towards the hills.
Anyone who climbs up those thick crusts
of land would ignore your flyer,

must be healthy and stick to local
produce. Avoid taxi after Uber
after taxi after e-scooter on our cut-

through street where shouts break out
when bumpers come to a head as no one
campaigns for it to be a one-way road.

Parking spaces as small as the recycling
boxes—I sidestep swear words
on my way to the veg store,

skip over clammy fists, wrap half a dozen carrots
in your leaflet—better than supermarket
plastic I suppose—to protect

them from the rain. A storm has arrived.
I can hear the high-pitched whistling from here:
another bottle clatters into the wall faster

than your deliveries, missing tyres
and late-night tiffs—an aggressive dip
with your pepperoni?

Your fast food doesn't shave time.
I design meals for a week at once you see,
avoid the next morning's belt battle,

I'm as active as traffic on our leafy city street—
still escape to the hills.

Cold Crooks by This Fire Pit

A pigeon naps by a dozing man,
their heads are tucked in. One to its chest,
the other under cardboard. How long

will they stay a duo by this fire pit?
These cold crooks thieving flames.
A chip wrapper folds in wind.

Whose meal was that—and when's the next?
It must be hard to live without respite.
Pigeon's feathers twitch, man's grunts

dampened by coats, one trainer beside his head.
A helicopter whirrs. Crew searches for convicts.
Nearby, a woman fist bumps anyone

in sight. She thumps of optimism, even
near this pit, as graffiti warns against the 9am-5pm.
Suits jest on their way to lunchtime drinks.

Pigeons fly up to 700 miles in a day—
more if they break their trip. This one chose
to doze here. Still half a day to go.

Today I Met an Armed Robber

a torturer, survivor, the cursed, the blessed,
the loved, and it took me the length of a queue
to know it. They are in the supermarket balancing items,
overweight baskets. As I sip my free Americano,
I guess who is who based on their posture, accent.
The torturer passes me a plastic bag.
The cursed smiles at a young girl, the blessed leaves
without paying. The armed robber and survivor saunter,
hand in hand—are they loved? The cashier studies me.
Doesn't even ask if I have a loyalty card.

You Are Here, Grandad, in This Mute Play Park

You hold my gaze over an empty playground
as you perch on a swing. Rockers spring,
monkey bars hang in sleet. Wind hoists
a chew bar wrapper, howling from time

to time. I scout for a bottle opener;
absent in this holiday let. I knock on every door
in the block, the last one at the very top proves a hit—
with a family troupe of boots outside.

An old man answers, fetches an opener, shakes my hand,
asks if I've just moved in. *Just here
for a few nights actually, cheers.*
His warmth stalks me down the hall.

When I leave into the lung-tugging frost,
I force the stuttering gate. Skip past you,
crouched on the merry-go-round. I'll explore the museum
and galleries, wrapped head to knees in tartan,

beanie hat—like the one I wore as a child.
I miss visiting the city to see you.
Remember that last time? I was 28 and punters
in a local bar parted to let you pass.

Before that, I took you to a pub
one afternoon at my university,
you told me all about my dad when he was a student—
long hair and calls from his landlord about the state

of his house. Now I'm sat in a bare playpark,
dirt spreading from a sandbox in this storm.
I could freeze the slide with my spit.
The entrance to the block is broken,

the access button pulled off the wall.
You always opened doors for me.
Would you be proud of me now, even now?
With bottle opener in hand,

I attempt the climbing net.
If I squint, I can spot you on the seesaw.

You Cry to Your Folks That I
Forced You to Carry Goalposts

Lambs' footprints climb fence posts,
snowmen lessened to leftovers;
mounds lie that had once formed heads.

We're six years old and our favourite ash,
beyond the gate, stretches like a dragon
guarding butternut skies.

Hills thaw as we're chased by chubbier kids,
dirty mags lie in the bushes next to the remnants
of bonfires. Our scarves in the branches

decorate ice-cream fields.
This afternoon in shin-high snow you sob
as we haul my goalposts home.

Three of us leapt high as hatchlings,
as if reaching for advent calendars.
With flakes tumbling, you caught the fence

with a hoop on your jeans' waist.
You dangle for a while
next to a small oak, then shout.

We turn but cheer too long to help
then brave the toughening slush,
our joyous tears try to glisten you free.

I don't remember a thank you,
just the sight of you upside down,
your torn jumper surrendering.

We all lug the goalposts back, but you blub
to your parents that I'd forced you to.
Your fingers drip by the open fire.

We huddle like twigs, our folks
only concerned that we shut the gate to keep
the lambs in. The last of snowmen melt.

Our (Third) Last Christmas at Bankside

The sale sign is up again,
I hear the knocking on the bank below.
These curtains do little to keep out the morning.

I waited years after we moved in
for the wall to be knocked down,
doubling the size of my room.

Geri Halliwell topped the charts,
we wore low hung jeans and tight,
long-sleeved tops with ripped holes for thumbs.

Our black and white timber home
peeks out from the hillside.
Grandad's roses by the door.

I kept my Nokia flip-phone in a box
under the bed when I was refused one,
paid £10 for it in the playground.

Rain knocks the window, no snow again this year.
Pages of my favourite novel
still stuck with bubblegum.

When I was presented with an MP3 player
one Christmas and spent the afternoon
downloading songs online,

my wheeled chair relentlessly rolling
along my uneven floor,
I received chat messages asking why

I was wasting a religious day,
that my parents were leading me
to the gates of hell.

Down the stairs now for brunch—
salmon on sourdough, sweet mustard sausages.
A knock on the door.

If only we could have gatherings
in my own home;
18 months later and not a room finished.

It is Mr and Mrs Grayson
for their annual bubbles.
As we sit around the kitchen table,

sweating from the hall fire,
I think how this is our third
last Christmas at my parents' house

and how I wish it never sells.

Christmas Eve in Our New Home on Elton Street

Needles grace others' flagstones,
this year bells wrap up their chimes and go,
the whippet's safe from alluring cloves.

No tinsel winks to festive hits,
we plant a makeshift tree; threadbare,
then baubles blossom, a star climbs.

Our Date Night Will Be Ponchos in January

with buckskin boots, plump cushions and a hoovered rug.
No broken toy trucks with scattered wheels,
no half-torn down Christmas tree
with its star dangling mid-branch.
No chalk scribbles along the skirting board
with splashes of spoilt milk.
Our night will be a Western,
where the protagonist falls for a peace-brokering barmaid
who refuses to serve those harbouring weapons,
quips over cornbread and whisky, how love is tougher than cacti.
No animated animals, nursery rhymes or gurgles,
no screams of *mama* or *baba* or *I want more, now!*
Our night will be a cowboy's favourite of fresh beef,
beans and fruit. Constant top ups, foot massages.
No leftovers from the kids' bowls that we battled
to make. No stumbling over train tracks, or nappy bags,
or puzzle pieces in our slippers.
Our night will be a poem better than this one.
With the world's greatest cowboy references.

Egg Lamp's Verdict

O judge of warmth, whether we
should cover our son's exposed fingers,
lay two blankets or one.

When we have parked our bodies for the night,
the ceiling glows
with your verdict: red for too warm.

Who are you to decide when we must drag
our sleepy mass to the cellar,
throw our wages at the heat meter

while our child murmurs in his sleep?
He smiles snuggly in stripes,
innocent as a hot water bottle.

We wish for unbroken rest, but treasure
morning hugs, his wisps of hair,
pudding cheeks as he gurgles.

His presence perfume-soft
while the walls
wear your ice-blue shade.

Here's Your Star Sticker Back
for Laith

I steal a star
sticker from your bedroom
wall and hide
it in my wallet.

You point at my back pocket
as it glows. I used to win
them for high marks at school.

Every time I treat myself to a coconut slice,
I see your star
and think how you shine in swim class,
of your husky new giggle.

When we share the night
sky and spot a shooting star,
that's
the one

passing
from you to I,
our time together:
me handing it back to you.

Let Me Breathe Apricots

When all is done in this fruit bowl of life
and there's nothing
left to grind,
let me breathe apricots into the winter sun,

so I may wake warmed in spring
to find hands rise again, surplus skin
stripped; pruned honey—
a dishful of dawn.

Acknowledgments

I am very grateful to family (Mum, Dad, Matt, Maddy, the Tahas and our inspiring kids), friends, editors and poets who have supported me. Namely, Vicky Morris, Anna Saunders, Matthew MC Smith, Stuart McPherson, Isabelle Kenyon, Tess Jolly and Andy Brown, who read and commented on these poems.

I'd like to thank the organisers and judges of the Canterbury Festival Poet of the Year Competition 2023 for shortlisting earlier versions of "Shove Your 3-for-2 Flyer" and "You Cry to Your Folks That I Forced You to Carry Goalposts." The Shelley Memorial Prize Poetry Competition 2022, for awarding third prize to a previous version of "Ode to a Rubber Pufferfish." Also, The Winged Moon for its monthly competition commendation of "The Sea Steals Our Picnic Blanket."

My thanks to Hiram Larew for publishing "Cold Crooks by This Fire Pit" on Poetry X Hunger. The initiative he founded uses poetry to raise awareness, compassion and funding for anti-hunger organisations.

I was privileged to be part of the 2024-2025 Literature Works' Word Space programme for writers in South West England. My special thanks to Helen Chaloner and my mentor Greta Stoddart.

Thank you to John Taylor and Midsomer Norton Stanza, who have been very accommodating in letting me join sessions online. Also, to BBC Radio Bristol for inviting me to the White Room Studio to read and discuss poems and the city's thriving poetry scene.

Finally, a big heartfelt thanks to staff in the neurosurgery ward at Southmead Hospital and the Hospital at Home service for making my stay and recovery as comfortable as possible. To former neurosurgeon Dr Charles Winter, for bringing me poetry and novels.

Some poems in this collection, or previous versions thereof, have appeared in the following publications:

Ode to a Rubber Pufferfish - *Shelley Memorial Project*

Ode to the Pruning Woman Eaten by Vines - *Magma*

My Son Grows as I Regress - *The Winged Moon*

We Meet in Attic Bar for My Stag Do - *Steel Jackdaw*

After Leaving the Ward - *The Wee Sparrow Poetry Press*

I Drown During an Awards Do as the Queen Dies - *Prole*

Shove Your 3-for-2 Flyer; You Cry to Your Folks That I Forced You to Carry Goalposts - *Canterbury Festival*

The View From This Hospital Window - *Ink, Sweat & Tears*

Why I Wear My Past to Work - *Sidhe Press*

Revellers Howl in the Fine Hours - *The Broken Spine*

Cold Crooks by This Fire Pit - *Poetry X Hunger*

The Sea Steals Our Picnic Blanket; Watching My Wife at Three Cliffs Bay; Here's Your Star Sticker Back - *Flight of the Dragonfly*

Christmas Eve in Our New Home on Elton Street - *Black Bough Poetry*

Founded in Atlanta, Georgia in 2023, PARLYAREE PRESS is dedicated to publishing writing that expands, reveals, and interrogates the mainstream. We seek out fiction, creative nonfiction, and poetry that exists in the liminal space between what was and what will be.

The cant of circus performers, freaks, queers, and thespians, Parlyaree is the invented language required to tell the stories of those othered, to keep their secrets, to keep them safe. It is a polyglot of experiences that may only be told in one's own voice. Parlyaree—as an invented language—borrows from what was to create something new.

That is what excites us at Parlyaree Press. Stories that transform; essays that reimagine; poetry that takes us behind the stanza to the core of our being and back again; language that plays as much as it conveys.

Writers: tell us your secrets.
Readers: reimagine your worlds.

www.ingramcontent.com/pod-product-compliance
Lightning Source LLC
Chambersburg PA
CBHW011219120626
46545CB00008B/3061